The Pool Frog

by Rachel Russ

illustrated by Adriana Puglisi

OXFORD
UNIVERSITY PRESS

It was the morning of the class trip.

Azeem was waiting for Finn.
Finn did not get on the coach.

"Finn is ill," said Miss Booth.

A man met them at the pond.

Amber put her net in the pond.

It was just some weeds.

“Fish need weeds,” said Oliver. “Weeds keep fish hidden.”

Then Azeem held up his net.

"A pool frog!" said Oliver.
"I have never seen one."

The next week, Finn was better.

"I love frogs!" said Finn.
"I wish I had been there."

Miss Booth took the children to the garden.

Now I can pond dip!
Cool!

Finn bent down to look.

That is just as good as a pool frog!

Pool Frogs

Pool frogs are hard to spot.
Pool frogs love to sit in the sun.

Encourage students to read the information about pool frogs then talk about it together.